THE COLD WAR

SIMON ADAMS

W

FRANKLIN WATTS
LONDON • SYDNEY

Illustrations   David Frankland

Designer   Billin Design Solutions
Editor   Caroline Brooke Johnson
Art Direction   Jason Anscomb
Editor-in-Chief   John C. Miles

© 2001 Franklin Watts

First published in 2001
by Franklin Watts
96 Leonard Street
London
EC2A 4XD

Franklin Watts Australia
56 O'Riordan Street
Alexandria
NSW 2015

ISBN 0 7496 4247 5

Dewey classification: 327

A CIP catalogue record
for this book is available
from the British Library.

Printed in Hong Kong/China

CONTENTS

End of World War II

On 25 April 1945, the US and Soviet armies met in Germany for the first time in the war against Nazi oppression. Their two armies had fought their way across Europe from opposite sides of the continent. Together they had won the war; now they had to win the peace.

"East and West have met… The forces of liberation have joined hands."

Radio commentator, 25 April 1945

DIVIDING THE WORLD

The defeat of Germany and Japan in 1945 at the end of World War II led to the division of Europe and Asia. The USA, with its French and British allies, controlled western Europe and the western half of both Germany and Austria, as well as South-East Asia, Japan, southern Korea and the islands of the Pacific Ocean. The USSR controlled eastern Germany and Austria, the rest of central and eastern Europe and northern Korea.

OPPOSITE SIDES

In 1945, the USA and the USSR (the Union of the Soviet Socialist Republics, or the Soviet Union, commonly known as Russia) were the two most powerful nations on earth. Yet they could not have been more different. The USA had a strong capitalist economy and a firm belief in the freedom of its people. The USSR was the world's first Communist country, formed in the Revolution of 1917. Led by its powerful and ruthless leader, Josef Stalin, the country had changed from a backward agricultural country into a leading industrial state in 25 years. But that change had been achieved at a huge cost in lives: peasants were forced on to state-run farms and opponents of the government were executed or sent to prison camps.

A Red Army soldier raises the Soviet flag on the ruins of the Reichstag – Germany's Parliament building – in 1945.

From left to right: Stalin, Roosevelt and Churchill.

WORLD WAR II

• 1939 – War breaks out in September; in 1940 most of Europe falls under German or Italian control

• 1941 – The war becomes global when Germany invades the USSR in June, and Japan attacks the USA in December. During 1943 Germany, Italy and Japan lose ground to the Allies – US, Soviet and British armies

• 1944 – In June, Allied troops invade France. As they advance eastwards, Soviet troops press westwards, dividing the continent in two

• 1945 – The war in Europe ends with Germany's surrender in May. Three months later, Japan surrenders after atomic bombs are dropped on two cities

• It is thought that 55 million people are killed in battle or on the home front. The USSR alone loses more than 20 million people. More than six million Jews and other minorities are murdered by the Nazis in the Holocaust

THE "BIG THREE"

The three Allied leaders – US President Franklin Roosevelt (1882–1945), Soviet leader Josef Stalin (1879–1953) and British Prime Minister Winston Churchill (1874–1965) – met in Tehran, Persia, in November 1943 and at Yalta, Russia, in February 1945 to agree the conduct of the war.

In April 1945, Harry Truman became US President after Roosevelt's death, while Clement Attlee replaced Churchill as British Prime Minister after winning the general election in July. In July–August, Truman, Attlee and Stalin met in the Berlin suburb of Potsdam to discuss the future of Europe.

CHAOTIC WORLD
Across Europe and Asia the old political system was in ruins. Many countries had no effective government. Towns and cities had been destroyed, and millions of refugees camped out in makeshift shelters. The fighting was over, but the task of rebuilding was huge. Both the USA and the USSR now had the chance to shape the world in their own image.

Start of the Cold War

The end of World War II left US, British and French troops controlling western Europe and Soviet troops controlling eastern Europe. In the West, democratic governments were re-established, but in eastern Europe a different picture emerged.

EASTERN BLOC

The USSR wanted to make sure that it was never again threatened by a powerful Germany. Along its western borders the Soviets set up a "buffer zone" of Communist countries between it and the West. Communist parties in each country received support from the USSR, overwhelming their political opponents by force or intimidation. In one country after another, Communist parties took full control.

By 1949 one-party Communist states were in place across eastern Europe, with three important exceptions.

In Greece a vicious civil war between the Communists and the royalist government ended in victory for the government. In Yugoslavia, the Communist government of Josip Broz (Tito) broke free from the USSR in 1948. During the war, Tito's partisans had liberated Yugoslavia from Nazi rule with limited outside help and they did not want to fall under Soviet domination.

In Austria the four war-time Allies (the USA, USSR, Great Britain and France) removed their troops in 1955, and the country became officially neutral.

Winston Churchill (with US President Harry Truman, left) on the way to deliver his "Iron Curtain" speech in Fulton, Missouri.

"From Stettin in the Baltic to Trieste in the Adriatic, an Iron Curtain has descended across the continent."

Winston Churchill, 5 March 1946

COLD WAR BEGINS

Many people feared that Communist control would spread to the West. They began to talk of a "Cold War" — a war of ideas and propaganda — between the two sides. In a 1946 speech, Winston Churchill said Europe was divided by an "Iron Curtain".

In 1949, therefore, 11 western nations set up the North Atlantic Treaty Organization (NATO) to link their armed forces. In 1955, the Eastern Bloc countries set up the Warsaw Pact.

THE SOVIET TAKE-OVER

- 1945 – Soviet troops occupy eastern Europe

- 1946 – Communist parties take full control of Bulgaria, followed by Romania and Poland in 1947, Czechoslovakia and Hungary in 1948

- 1947 – Eastern Bloc rejects Marshall Aid from the USA and in 1949 sets up COMECON – Council for Mutual Economic Assistance – which ties eastern economies to the USSR

- 1949 – The German Democratic Republic is set up in eastern Germany

- 1955 – USSR and its allies sign the Warsaw Pact, establishing a unified military command in eastern Europe

MOLOTOV

Vyacheslav Molotov (1890–1986) was Prime Minister of the USSR from 1930–41 and Foreign Minister from 1939–49 and from 1953–56. Devoted to Stalin, he worked hard to ensure total Soviet control over eastern Europe. He negotiated treaties with each Communist country, binding them to the USSR, and became known as "Mr No" in the West since he refused to compromise with western nations.

First confrontations

On 12 March 1947, President Truman addressed Congress about the spread of Communism. He committed the USA "to support free peoples who are resisting attempted subjugation by . . . outside pressures". In other words, this meant stopping Communism from spreading throughout the world.

"I believe it must be the policy of the United States to support free peoples."

President Harry Truman, 12 March 1947

TRUMAN DOCTRINE
The Truman Doctrine, as this key commitment was called, marked the real beginning of the Cold War.

Promising to help any country threatened by a Communist take-over, the US government gave $400 million to Greece and Turkey to keep them free of Communist control. The USA was fighting a new global war, this time against its old ally, the USSR.

RECOVERY PLANS
The first step in this war was to support the recovery and rebuilding of war-torn European economies.

The task was urgent: according to the US Secretary of State, George Marshall, "the patient is sinking while the doctors deliberate". Marshall put together a vast programme of aid "to restore the confidence of the European peoples in the economic future of their own countries and of Europe as a whole . . . Our policy is directed not against any country but against hunger, poverty, desperation and chaos."

DIVIDED BERLIN

Germany was the most desperate place. In 1945 it was divided by the war-time Allies into four occupation zones. The capital, Berlin was also divided into four.

The USSR wanted to keep Germany divided and take much of its industry and wealth to the USSR to repair some of the damage that the German armies had caused there during the war. The USA, Britain and France wanted to use Marshall Aid to rebuild Germany as a modern, peaceful, pro-western state.

EAST AND WEST

These differences came to a head in 1948. The three western Allies agreed to merge their zones into a unified West Germany and introduced a new currency for West Berlin — controlled by the Western Allies but now geographically isolated in Soviet-occupied territory.

The USSR retaliated by introducing its own currency in East Berlin and blocked road and rail access to the city from the West through Soviet-occupied East Germany. West Berlin was now cut off.

THE BERLIN AIRLIFT

The western Allies responded to this threat by airlifting in supplies. Between 26 June 1948 and 12 May 1949, the USA and Britain organized 277,264 flights, bringing in food, clothing, coal and even cigarettes. Planes landed in the city every 90 seconds, carrying up to 13,000 tonnes of supplies a day.

The situation was tense, but in 1949 the USSR backed down. The blockade of West Berlin came to an end, and both Germany and Berlin were formally divided into the pro-western Federal Republic and the Communist German Democratic Republic.

Food and other supplies are unloaded during the Berlin Airlift.

265414

FACT FILE

THE MARSHALL PLAN

• June 1947 – US Secretary of State George Marshall proposes a European Recovery Program – nicknamed the Marshall Plan – to help European nations rebuild their shattered post-war economies

• The plan is supported enthusiastically by western nations; the USSR rejects the plan, as do eastern Europe, Spain and Finland

• Between 1948–52 the USA gives more than $13,700 million in aid (that is about $130,000 million today). Britain gets $3,200 million, France gets $2,700 million and Iceland gets $29 million – the smallest amount

• Most aid is given in commodities such as grain, industrial machinery or even mules, which are sent to help farmers in northern Greece

• Marshall Aid restores the European economy and ties western Europe – economically and politically – to the USA. Because the Eastern Bloc refuses to accept aid, it confirms the division of Europe into East and West

The Korean War

Refugees flee the fighting during the Korean War.

At the end of World War II, the Japanese colony of Korea – a peninsula off the north-east coast of China – was occupied by Soviet and US troops. Within five years, the Cold War became hot as war erupted in Korea.

A DIVIDED COUNTRY

At the Yalta Conference of February 1945, the wartime Allies agreed to divide Korea temporarily along the 38th parallel until the country was reunified. Soviet troops occupied the North, US troops the South. Unification never happened, and in 1948 both Communist North and pro-Western South Korea became independent. Each state claimed authority over the other. During 1949, tension increased.

In the South fears of a Communist take-over increased when Communists under Mao Zedong finally took control of China in October 1949 after years of civil war. Under the leadership of Kim Il Sung, North Korea pressed the USSR and China to support its invasion of the South to reunify the country. Both countries gave their approval, but neither wanted to be involved in any fighting.

THE WAR

The North Korean attack began on 25 June 1950 and caught South Korea totally by surprise. US troops had withdrawn from South Korea in 1949 and the South Koreans were no match for the heavily armed forces of the North. Within two months, North Korean troops had pushed the South's army almost into the sea.

WESTERN AID

Western governments quickly came to South Korea's aid. The United Nations (UN) condemned the invasion and sent a multi-national force led by US General Douglas MacArthur, with troops from the USA, Britain, Australia and 12 other countries. The first troops landed in July. In September, MacArthur launched a massive amphibious assault at Inchon, behind enemy lines, and pressed north towards the Chinese border. China, alarmed that the US might invade, sent 180,000 troops into Korea. They soon drove the UN troops south again. MacArthur wanted to bomb China to force it to withdraw, but President Truman refused. As the fighting stabilized around the old border, he sacked MacArthur for defying his authority.

ARMISTICE

The war ground on for another two years before an armistice was eventually signed, bringing peace to the divided country. In total, perhaps two million soldiers and up to two million Korean civilians lost their lives. No peace treaty was ever signed, and it was not until 2000 that the leaders of North and South Korea met for the first time in an attempt to settle their differences.

TRUMAN

Harry Truman (1884–1972) was elected Vice-President of the USA in 1944, but within 11 weeks of taking office, he became President following the death of Franklin Roosevelt on 12 April 1945. Truman had little experience of foreign affairs, but he quickly took control. He authorized the use of atomic bombs to end the war against Japan and took a strong line with the USSR over its expansion into eastern Europe.

In 1948 President Truman stood for re-election and won a big victory. In 1949 he took the USA into NATO, the first peacetime military alliance the US had ever entered, and sent US troops to fight in Korea in 1950. He retired from office in 1953.

"There is no substitute for victory."
US General Douglas MacArthur, 20 March 1951

THE KOREAN WAR

- **June 1950** – North Korean troops invade South Korea, capturing its capital, Seoul

- **July 1950** – First UN troops arrive in Korea under General Douglas MacArthur but are quickly pushed back

- **September 1950** – UN troops land at Inchon, behind North Korean lines

- **October 1950** – UN troops invade North Korea and capture Pyongyang, its capital, and head for the Chinese border; first Chinese troops enter Korea

- **November 1950** – Chinese troops launch massive assault

- **January 1951** – North Korean and Chinese troops retake Seoul

- **March 1951** – Fighting stabilizes around the old border between North and South

- **April 1951** – Truman sacks MacArthur for repeatedly advocating war against China

- **July 1951** – Talks begin about a ceasefire

- **July 1953** – Armistice is finally signed at Panmunjom, ending the war and dividing Korea roughly along its old border

The Arms Race

In 1945 the USA exploded the world's first atomic bombs. Four years later the USSR exploded its first nuclear weapon. The Cold War now had the potential to turn into a devastating world war, killing millions of people.

> ## "Whoever gains the ultimate supremacy of space gains ultimate control over the Earth."
> **US military adviser, 1958**

THE RACE BEGINS

When the USA exploded its three bombs in 1945 — one was tested in the New Mexico desert, two were dropped on the Japanese cities of Hiroshima and Nagasaki — it was the only country that had the technological know-how to produce such weapons. This gave the USA an immense advantage over the USSR: it alone could threaten to use the bomb if the Cold War turned into a real war.

That advantage, however, was short-lived. Stalin ordered Soviet scientists to catch up with the USA, a process the Americans thought would take them eight years. The Soviets did it in four. The first atomic bombs were fission bombs, which split plutonium or uranium atoms to create an explosion. The new generation would be fusion bombs, which fused hydrogen atoms together for a more devastating result.

THE H-BOMB

The USA tested its first H-bomb on 1 November 1952 on the tiny Pacific island of Eniwetok. The bomb was 1,000 times more powerful than the bomb dropped on Hiroshima. Nine months later the USSR exploded a technically superior H-bomb. Over the next decade, each side exploded more advanced bombs as the nuclear race hotted up.

Other nations joined in too: Britain exploded an atomic bomb in 1952, as did France in 1960 and China in 1964. By 1968 all three had tested their own H-bombs. Around the world the number of nuclear weapons grew massively: the USA had 298 in 1950, 27,100 in 1962.

The first nuclear weapons were designed to be dropped from aircraft, but on

15 May 1957, the USSR tested the world's first intercontinental ballistic missile (ICBM), capable of carrying a nuclear warhead. Five months later, on 5 October 1957, it launched *Sputnik*, the world's first artificial satellite, into space.

THE SPACE RACE

The launch of *Sputnik* alarmed the Americans, because they realized that the USA was slipping behind the USSR in scientific achievement. They also realized that Soviet nuclear missiles would soon be able to threaten US cities. As a result, the USA rapidly increased its nuclear capability and soon tested its own ICBMs and intermediate-range ballistic missiles (IRBMs). Most importantly, it established the National Aeronautics and Space Administration (NASA) in 1958.

Three years later President Kennedy pledged to land an American on the Moon. The race for nuclear supremacy was now joined by a race to reach the Moon, a race won by the Americans in 1969.

THE SPACE RACE

- 1903 – Russia develops idea of space rockets fuelled by liquefied gas

- 1926 – America launches first liquid-fuelled rocket

- 1944 – German scientist Wernher von Braun develops V-2 rockets; he later works for the USA

- 1957 – Soviets launch *Sputnik*, the first satellite in space

- 1958 – USA launches its first satellite, *Explorer I*

- 1959 – Soviet *Luna 2* probe is the first spacecraft to land on the Moon

- 1961 – Soviet cosmonaut Yuri Gagarin becomes the first person in space on 12 April; US astronaut Alan Shepard follows a month later

- 1965 – Soviet cosmonaut Alexei Leonov is the first person to walk in space

- 1966 – Soviet *Luna 9* is first craft to land on the Moon

- 1969 – US astronaut Neil Armstrong becomes first person to walk on the Moon

- 1998 – Work starts on the International Space Station, a joint venture between the USA, Russia and others

Potent symbol of the Cold War – Moscow's annual May Day parade.

The Berlin Wall

The death of Stalin in March 1953 had a huge impact throughout eastern Europe. Now that Stalin had gone, reformers hoped that Communist governments would relax their harsh rule and introduce peaceful reforms.

The government refused to negotiate and used Soviet troops to crush the uprising. More than 40 workers were killed and thousands of strike leaders arrested. Anti-government riots in Czechoslovakia and strikes in Hungary and Romania were also suppressed.

SOCIALISM WITH A HUMAN FACE

Hopes for change grew when Nikita Khrushchev became the new Soviet leader. He introduced "socialism with a human face" and overturned many of Stalin's oppressive policies, releasing political prisoners and making life easier for working people. Abroad, he improved relations with China and Yugoslavia and made visits to India and other non-aligned countries.

In 1955, the USSR agreed with its three war-time Allies to withdraw all troops from Austria in return for Austrian neutrality. At a secret session of the 20th Congress of the Soviet Communist party in February 1956, Khrushchev denounced Stalin as a "capricious, irritable and brutal" leader who had made many mistakes.

The speech had a dramatic impact across eastern Europe. In June 1956 workers in Poland demanded reform. Khrushchev threatened to send in Soviet troops, but Poland won limited independence providing it remained loyal to the USSR. In Hungary, however, the rapid pace of change alarmed Khrushchev, who crushed its attempt to achieve democratic reform.

Troops stand guard as the Berlin Wall is built.

THE THAW

The first people to press for change were the East Germans. Their government demanded that workers work harder for no increase in pay. In June 1953 popular demonstrations broke out, and more than 400,000 workers went on strike.

> ## "Whether you like it or not, history is on our side. We will bury you."
> Nikita Khrushchev, 18 November 1956

THE WALL

After the failure of the Hungarian rising, the Iron Curtain remained firmly closed across Europe. The one exception was Berlin. Here, East Germans could cross freely into West Berlin, where they saw the freedoms and higher standard of living enjoyed in the West. As a result, 2.8 million East Germans fled west between 1949–61, one-sixth of the entire population.

Many were skilled workers, whose loss seriously weakened the East German economy.

In 1961, the East German leaders decided to act. On Sunday 13 August, workers began to build a 165-km (103-mile) barbed-wire barrier around West Berlin. Much of this soon turned into a solid wall. In June 1963, US President John Kennedy visited Berlin.

In a speech, he declared that "all free men . . . are citizens of Berlin, and therefore as a free man, I take pride in the words 'Ich bin ein Berliner [I am a Berliner]'." Many smiled because a Berliner was a popular local doughnut! More seriously, the Wall now became the symbol of the division of the world into East and West, and of the Cold War itself.

KHRUSHCHEV

Nikita Khrushchev (1894–1971) served in the Red Army in the civil war that followed the 1917 Russian Revolution and rose rapidly through the ranks of the Communist party. On Stalin's death in 1953, he became party First Secretary and then Prime Minister in 1958. He was removed from office in 1964.

Khrushchev had no formal education but he had a very quick mind. He was a strong and capable leader who did much to reform and modernize the USSR. He was determined that the USSR should overtake the USA as the world's most advanced nation. However, he sometimes miscalculated the effects his policies would have, notably in eastern Europe and Cuba.

The Cuban Missile Crisis

The greatest threat to world peace during the Cold War came from the island of Cuba, just 145 km (90 miles) off the southern coast of the USA. For two weeks in 1962 the world stood on the brink of nuclear war.

CUBAN REVOLUTION

The USA had dominated Cuba ever since it had helped the island win its independence from Spain in 1898. Since 1933 Cuba had been ruled by the corrupt Fulgencio Batista. American firms owned most of the land and industry. Most Cubans hated Batista, and many joined the guerrilla campaign, begun in 1956 by Fidel Castro, to rid Cuba of Batista. On 8 January 1959, Castro took power.

At first, Castro did little to upset the USA. But in February 1960, he signed a trade agreement with the USSR. He also nationalized many US-owned companies. In retaliation the USA imposed an economic blockade on Cuba, refusing to sell it petrol or buy its sugar, Cuba's main export. Cuba was now totally dependent on the USSR for all its vital supplies, a situation that would have grave consequences.

> **"I call upon Khrushchev to halt and eliminate this clandestine, reckless and provocative threat to world peace."**
>
> President John Kennedy, 22 October 1962

This US spy plane photograph shows a Russian ship approaching Cuba with crated nuclear bomber aircraft on its deck.

FAILED INVASION

The USA became very alarmed by this revolutionary government off its coast and began to arm and train anti-Castro Cubans in exile in central America. With help from the US Central Intelligence Agency (CIA), they landed in Cuba on 17 April 1961 at the Bay of Pigs, but the invasion was a total failure as no Cubans rallied to their cause.

MISSILE CRISIS

On 14 October 1962, a US U-2 spy plane photographed a Soviet missile site under construction in Cuba. On 22 October US President Kennedy announced a total naval blockade of Cuba and demanded that the USSR remove its nuclear missiles and stop supplying new ones. The USA then prepared to invade the island. The world held its breath as the two powers appeared to be on the brink of nuclear war.

RESOLUTION

The USSR refused to remove its missiles unless the USA withdrew its missiles from Turkey — which directly threatened the USSR itself. After several days of tense negotiations, a deal was reached on 28 October. The USSR agreed to remove its missiles from Cuba in return for the USA ending its blockade and agreeing not to invade the island. As agreed, the USA quietly removed its missiles from Turkey the following year. The threat of nuclear war lifted as both sides decided to compromise rather than risk a confrontation.

KENNEDY

John Fitzgerald Kennedy (1917–63) served as a Congressman for Massachusetts and then in the US Senate before being elected US President in 1960, the youngest-ever elected President and the first Roman Catholic. He was strongly anti-Communist and campaigned for President on a programme of increasing US defences against the USSR.

In office, he was an inspiring leader. He held his nerve during the Cuban missile crisis and signed the Nuclear Test Ban Treaty of 1963 with the USSR and Britain, ending the testing of nuclear weapons in the air, under water or in space. At home, he tried to get rid of the worst forms of racial and social injustice. He was assassinated in mysterious circumstances in Dallas, Texas, on 22 November 1963.

AROUND THE WORLD

The Cold War was fought in every continent of the world:

- 1947 – Central and South American nations sign anti-Communist Rio Pact with USA

- 1954 – South-East Asian Treaty Organization set up to curb Communism

- 1954 – USA supports coup against left-wing government of Guatemala

- 1955 – Four Middle East nations sign Baghdad Pact (renamed CENTO) against USSR

- 1962 – Cuban crisis

- 1965 – USA prevents Communist take-over of the Dominican Republic

- 1967, 1973 – USA supports Israel, USSR the Arabs in two Arab-Israeli wars

- 1973 – USA backs coup in Chile against the elected Marxist President Allende

- 1975 – USA and USSR support different sides in Angolan civil war

- 1977 – USSR supports Ethiopia, USA backs Somalia in desert war

- 1980s – USA supports Contra rebels against elected left-wing government of Nicaragua

- 1983 – USA invades Grenada to remove its left-wing government

War in Vietnam

For over 30 years, the South-East Asian country of Vietnam was at war. At first it fought for its independence from French and Japanese colonial rule, but during the 1960s and 1970s it was the scene of the Cold War's biggest military confrontation.

> **"A poor feudal nation had beaten a great colonial power ... It meant a lot; not just to us but to people all over the world."**
>
> Viet Minh leader General Vo Nguyen Giap, 1954

A DIVIDED COUNTRY

The Vietnamese campaign for independence from French rule began in the 1920s. When the Japanese occupied the country in 1941, the Communist revolutionary leader, Ho Chi Minh, formed the Viet Minh movement to fight for independence. In 1945, he declared Vietnam independent, but the French returned.

After a long war, the French were defeated in 1954. The French agreed to leave, but the country was now divided, with the Communists of Ho Chi Minh ruling the North, and pro-Western forces ruling the South.

A young US soldier peers from thick jungle in Vietnam.

A NEW WAR

The new government of South Vietnam was very harsh. In 1960, the National Front for the Liberation of South Vietnam, or Viet Cong, was formed to fight for unification under Northern rule. By 1964 it looked as if the Viet Cong might win.

In August 1964 US and North Vietnamese naval ships clashed off Vietnam. This gave the USA the excuse it needed to join the war. President Johnson persuaded Congress to authorize "all necessary steps, including the use of armed forces".

USA JOINS WAR

US forces poured into Vietnam, and in February 1965 US planes began to bomb the north. By the end of 1966, the USA had more than 400,000 troops in Vietnam, but the Viet Cong and North Vietnamese were skilled fighters. Led by General Giap, they almost seized the southern capital, Saigon, during the Tet Offensive of 1968.

At home, many Americans protested against the war, and international criticism of the USA's involvement grew.

PEACE AT LAST

In 1968 the USA and North Vietnam opened peace talks in Paris. The USA built up the South Vietnamese army and slowly withdrew its own troops. By the time a ceasefire was agreed in January 1973, all US troops had left Vietnam. For the next two years, the South struggled to survive, but in April 1975 North Vietnamese forces entered Saigon and reunified Vietnam.

Although the USA had lost the war, it had avoided direct conflict with either the USSR or China.

HO CHI MINH

Ho Chi Minh ("Ho, the seeker of light") (1890–1969) was a school teacher. In 1918 he moved to Paris, where he campaigned for Vietnamese independence from French rule and became a founder-member of the French Communist party. In 1940 he organized an uprising in Vietnam. When that failed, he fled to southern China, where he set up the Viet Minh independence movement.

After Japan's defeat in 1945, Ho Chi Minh declared North Vietnam independent and fought an eight-year war to expel the French. When the French withdrew in 1954 and Vietnam was split in two, he led the fight against South Vietnam to unify his country. In 1975 Saigon, the former capital of South Vietnam, was renamed Ho Chi Minh City in his honour.

Détente

Throughout the 1960s and 1970s, the two superpowers – the USA and USSR – tried to put aside their differences. They formed a détente, or understanding, with each other. The results were not always successful, but it reduced the threat of war.

> "The Cold War has outlived itself and there is need for a new, sensible and realistic policy."
>
> **Soviet leader Leonid Brezhnev, May 1975**

ARMS LIMITATION

By the early 1960s the USA and the USSR each had enough nuclear weapons to destroy all life on the planet. Both sides spent vast sums of money on weapons they hoped never to use. Their value was to deter both sides from starting a war.

Many people objected to nuclear weapons on moral as well as military and economic grounds. In Britain, thousands of people marched in protest each year or joined the Campaign for Nuclear Disarmament (CND). Politicians, too, started to question the amount of money being spent on nuclear weapons.

NUCLEAR TREATIES

In 1963 the USA, USSR and Britain signed the first-ever nuclear treaty – the Nuclear Test Ban Treaty – which prohibited all but underground nuclear tests. In 1968 the three signed the Nuclear Non-Proliferation Treaty, preventing the spread of nuclear technology to other countries. The other two nuclear powers – France and China – did not sign either treaty. A further advance was made in 1972, when the USA and USSR signed the far-reaching Strategic Arms Limitation Talks (SALT) Agreement. For the first time, they agreed to limit the number of nuclear weapons each possessed.

A protester faces tanks during the "Prague Spring" of 1968.

NEED FOR DÉTENTE

Both the USA and the USSR needed better relations with each other and the rest of the world. The USA was unpopular because of the Vietnam War, while the USSR was unpopular because it invaded Czechoslovakia in 1968 in order to end "socialism with a human face".

The USSR, too, was concerned by the growing power of Communist China. President Nixon exploited this rift between the two Communist giants when he became the first US President ever to visit China in February 1972. Later that year Nixon visited the Soviet leader, Leonid Brezhnev, in Moscow, again a first for a US leader.

EUROPEAN MOVES

In Europe the new West German Chancellor, Willy Brandt, began a policy of *Ostpolitik*, or "east policy". He signed a non-aggression pact with the USSR in 1970 and concluded a treaty with Poland, recognizing its borders and thus ending German claims to the land it lost at the end of World War II. In 1972 he signed a treaty with East Germany, recognizing its existence for the first time.

CLIMAX OF DÉTENTE

In 1975 in Helsinki, 33 European nations, as well as the USA and Canada, signed the Final Act of the Conference on Security and Co-operation in Europe. This treaty confirmed the existing borders of Europe and encouraged co-operation between all states.

THE PRAGUE SPRING

• January 1968 – Reformer Alexander Dubcek becomes First Secretary of the Czech Communist party

• March 1968 – Hard-line President Antonin Novotny resigns and is succeeded by reformer Ludvik Svoboda

• May–June 1968 – Many liberal reforms are introduced

• July 1968 – Czech government refuses to halt reforms; USSR halts the withdrawal of its troops after miitary exercises in the country

• 20 August 1968 – Warsaw Pact troops invade Czechoslovakia and arrest reform leaders, including Dubcek, who is taken to Moscow for talks

• October 1968 – Czech leaders agree to halt reform programme

• January 1969 – Jan Palach, a student, burns himself to death in Prague in a public protest against the Soviet occupation; demonstrations continue throughout the country

• April 1969 – Dubcek is deposed in favour of hardline Gustav Husak, ending the Prague Spring

Deep freeze

In the late 1970s, the process of détente came to a halt, and even went into reverse. For almost a decade, the Cold War raged on with increasing ferocity.

THE END OF DÉTENTE
The new Democrat President Jimmy Carter, elected in 1976, was tougher on the USSR over human rights issues than his Republican predecessors, Richard Nixon and Gerald Ford. The USSR believed that human rights were an internal matter, and objected to US interference.

Two events pushed relations between the two superpowers back into the deep freeze. Firstly, in 1977 the USSR installed new intermediate-range SS-20 missiles in Europe to replace some 20-year-old missiles. The USA and NATO saw this as a direct threat to peace in Europe and began to install intermediate-range Pershing II ballistic missiles and ground-launched cruise missiles in retaliation. Their total number was less than 600, but the USSR, too, saw them as a threat to peace. Many West Europeans agreed: huge demonstrations against the missiles took place across Europe throughout the early 1980s.

Secondly, on Christmas Day 1979 Soviet troops entered the central Asian state of Afghanistan to support the pro-Communist government against opposition Islamic rebels known as the Mujahedeen ("soldiers of God"), who objected to the government's policies of educating women and other reforms. The USSR was concerned that if the Afghan government lost control, an Islamic revolution could spread throughout central Asia and into the USSR itself.

Women peace campaigners protest at the deployment of US missiles in Britain.

REACTION

These two events ended any attempt at détente. US and other Western athletes boycotted the 1980 Olympic Games held in Moscow. Later that year, US electors voted in the Republican Ronald Reagan as President. Immediately, he increased defence spending by 50 per cent with the aim of defeating the USSR.

Reagan sent aid to the Mujahedeen in Afghanistan, funded the Contras — anti-government guerrillas — trying to overthrow the democratically elected left-wing government of Nicaragua, and proposed building an anti-missile system in space. Known as the Strategic Defence Initiative, and nicknamed "Star Wars" by its opponents, this system would have knocked out all incoming Soviet missiles in flight. In response, the Soviets threatened to build more missiles.

REAGAN

Ronald Reagan (b.1911) was a Hollywood film star before becoming governor of California from 1967–74. In 1980, he was elected President of the USA, the oldest person ever to hold the office. He was re-elected President in 1984, handing over to his Vice-President, George Bush, in 1989.

Ronald Reagan believed that the USA had a duty to lead the free world against Communism and that it must build up its defences to protect itself against the USSR. He was never very concerned about the details or implementation of his policies, which he left to his advisers, but he was an excellent down-to-earth communicator.

ARMS INTO PEACE

• 1977 — USSR places intermediate-range SS-20 missiles in Europe

• 1979 — USA locates intermediate-range cruise and Pershing ballistic missiles in Europe to counter the SS-20s

• 1979 — USA and USSR sign SALT II Treaty limiting a wide range of nuclear weapons but the treaty is never ratified

• 1981 — Massive anti-nuclear demonstrations across Europe

• 1983 — USA sets up the Strategic Defence Initiative ("Star Wars")

• 1986 — USSR proposes a 15-year timetable for the elimination of all nuclear weapons

• 1987 — USA and USSR agree to get rid of all intermediate-range nuclear weapons

• 1991 — USA and USSR agree Strategic Arms Reduction Treaty (START), reducing offensive long-range nuclear weapons by one-third

• 1993 — USA and USSR sign START II treaty, agreeing to further reductions and limiting their nuclear capacity to 3,500 strategic nuclear warheads each

Glasnost

On 10 March 1985 a new leader took control in the USSR. Mikhail Gorbachev was open to new ideas and wanted to break with the hard-line policies of the past.

ALL CHANGE

In November 1982 the ageing Soviet leader Leonid Brezhnev died. His two successors were old and ill – Yuri Andropov died in February 1984 and Konstantin Chernenko died in March 1985. They governed a country that lagged behind the USA and needed urgent reform.

Before Gorbachev took office, he stated in December 1984 that "profound transformations must be carried out in the economy and the entire system of social relations, and a qualitatively higher standard of living must be ensured for the Soviet people". He proposed to do this through a combination of *glasnost* – openness, or a free exchange of ideas and information – and *perestroika* – the reconstruction of the entire Soviet system.

Gorbachev toured the USSR, meeting ordinary people and asking for their views. He wanted to reform and update the existing Communist system, not replace it with something else.

> **"I like Mr Gorbachev. We can do business together."**
> Prime Minister Margaret Thatcher, December 1984

A new order in the USSR – Mikhail Gorbachev meets the people

A NEW FACE

Abroad, Gorbachev made an immediate impression. The British Prime Minister, Margaret Thatcher, soon recognized that Gorbachev was a new sort of leader. So, too, did US President Ronald Reagan. Gorbachev and Reagan met for the first time in Geneva, Switzerland, in November 1985. Gorbachev wanted to reduce Soviet military spending but felt threatened by the US proposals for Star Wars. The USA would not give way, but a friendly relationship between the two leaders was established.

END IN SIGHT

In January 1986 Gorbachev proposed that both countries aim for a nuclear-free world by 2000. He also began to withdraw Soviet troops from Afghanistan and pressured the Polish government to introduce economic and political reforms.

In the Icelandic capital of Reykjavik in October 1986 Gorbachev again met Reagan and came close to agreeing the destruction of all nuclear weapons within 10 years. This was a step too far for the USA, which did not want to abandon Star Wars, but in December 1987 the two sides did agree to get rid of all their intermediate-range nuclear missiles — the SS-20s, cruise and Pershing missiles — from Europe. This was the first time ever that an entire class of nuclear weapons had been abolished. The end of the Cold War was in sight.

GORBACHEV

Mikhail Gorbachev (b.1931) studied law at Moscow University before joining the Communist party in 1952. He swiftly rose through the party, making a name for himself as an open-minded reformer. He became leader in 1985 and soon embarked on a rapid programme of economic and social reform.

In 1988 he got rid of the last remaining hard-line Communists from his government and rewrote the Soviet constitution to allow non-Communists to stand for Parliament. In 1989 he was elected President of the USSR for five years.

However, his reforms weakened the USSR, and opposition to his rule grew from all sides. In August 1991, Communist hard-liners staged a coup against Gorbachev, which failed. However, he lost much of his power in the attempted coup, and had to leave office when the USSR collapsed on Christmas Day 1991. He won the Nobel Peace Prize in 1990.

SOLIDARITY IN POLAND

- **July 1980** – Rising food prices lead to strikes across Poland

- **August 1980** – Solidarity, an independent trade union led by electrician Lech Walesa, is set up in the Gdansk shipyards to demand reforms

- **August 1980** – Polish government allows independent trade unions

- **February 1981** – General Jaruzelski becomes Communist Prime Minister

- **April 1981** – Food rationing is introduced; strikes and protests continue

- **December 1981** – Martial (military) law is introduced. Solidarity leaders are imprisoned

- **July 1983** – Martial law ends, but Solidarity remains banned

- **April 1989** – Ban on Solidarity is lifted. It is allowed to contest the general election

- **June 1989** – Solidarity wins landslide victory

- **September 1989** – First non-Communist government in eastern Europe since 1948 takes power

- **December 1990** – Lech Walesa is elected President of Poland

End of the Cold War

On 7 December 1988 Mikhail Gorbachev addressed the United Nations in New York. He signalled the end of Soviet power in eastern Europe and cut the size of the Red Army by 500,000 men. No longer could repressive governments rely on Soviet forces to crush dissent.

"I do not regard the end of the Cold War as a victory for one side . . . The end of the Cold War is our common victory."

Mikhail Gorbachev, January 1992

REVOLUTION

Hungary and Poland were the first Eastern Bloc countries to allow the formation of opposition parties and set a date for multi-party elections. In September 1989, the first non-Communist government in eastern Europe since 1948 took power in Poland. Hungary also began to dismantle its fortified border with Austria, opening up a large gap in the Iron Curtain between East and West. Many East Germans poured through seeking a better life in West Germany.

WALL COMES DOWN

The East German government refused to relax its hard-line rule, but Gorbachev told them that change was on its way. Massive street protests broke out across East Germany and on 9 November the government opened its border. Thousands poured across the Berlin Wall to West Berlin, and Germans began to dismantle it.

On the same day as the Berlin Wall came down, a coup swept away the hard-line Communist government of Bulgaria. In Czechoslovakia the government resigned after massive protests.

Freedom – West Berliners help East Berliners over the Wall in 1989.

In December the dissident playwright and human-rights activist Václav Havel became President, with Alexander Dubcek, the leader of the Prague Spring, as speaker of the Federal Assembly. Czechoslovakia's "Velvet Revolution" had peacefully removed the Communists after 41 years in power.

The dictatorial Romanian leader, Nicolae Ceaucescu and his wife Elena tried to flee, but were caught, tried and executed on Christmas Day.

By the end of 1989 popular protests had removed every Communist government in eastern Europe.

USSR COLLAPSES

Inside the USSR unrest was growing in the 15 republics that made up the country. In August 1991, a group of hard-line Communists staged a coup to remove Gorbachev from power. He was held prisoner while resistance was organized by Russia's President, Boris Yeltsin.

The coup was defeated, and the Communist party, which had held power in the USSR since the 1917 Revolution, fell apart. Gorbachev now had little support. One by one, the individual republics declared their independence.

Gorbachev tried to reform the USSR to keep them together, but on Christmas Day 1991, he resigned as President and the USSR came to an end. At last the Cold War was over.

YELTSIN

Boris Yeltsin (b.1931) was born in western Siberia. He worked for the Communist party from 1968. In 1985, he became First Secretary of the Moscow party. At first, he tried to reform the Communist system from within, but he eventually left the party.

Yelstin was elected chairman of the Russian Soviet in May 1990 and President of Russia in 1991, gaining huge prestige when he defeated the attempted Communist coup against Gorbachev in August 1991. As President, he tried to introduce a Western-style market economy, but he was often erratic in his actions and many of his reforms failed. In 1994–95, he fought a vicious war against Chechen rebels. He retired in favour of his chosen successor, Vladimir Putin, in 2000.

Glossary

Allies, the	The USA, USSR, Britain and France, which fought together against Germany, Italy and Japan in World War II; often called the Four Powers.
Capitalism	An economic system based on the private ownership of industry, finance and property.
Chancellor	Prime Minister, or leader, of Germany.
Cold War	The war of words, ideas and propaganda between Communist countries and the Western world, which lasted from from 1945–91.
Communism	Belief in a society without different social classes in which everyone is equal and where all property is owned by the people.
Congress	The elected Parliament of the USA, divided into the lower House of Representatives and the upper Senate.
coup d'état	A sudden illegal or violent seizure of government by an opposition group.
democracy	Government by the people or their elected representatives, as in the USA or Britain.
détente	Friendship and understanding between East and West.
dissident	A person who dissents from or disagrees with the political system of a country.
Eastern Bloc	The Communist countries of eastern Europe, including the USSR.
federal	System of government, as in West Germany, where power is shared between national and state (local or regional) governments and individual states have considerable powers.
glasnost	The policy of "openness" in domestic affairs pursued by Gorbachev in the USSR.
hard line	A tough and unyielding policy or course of action.
Holocaust	The deliberate policy of the German Nazi party to kill Europe's Jews during World War II. More than six million people lost their lives, including many gypsies, homosexuals, trade unionists, Communists and other political opponents of Nazi Germany.
Iron Curtain	The phrase used by Winston Churchill in 1946 to describe the division of Europe into East and West.
market economy	An economy run on capitalist lines in which there is little or no intervention or control by the government, as in the USA.

National Socialist (Nazi) party	The extreme political party led by Adolf Hitler which controlled Germany from 1933–45. The Nazis believed in the supremacy of the German people and tried to kill all Jews and other people they considered to be racially or politically inferior.
NATO	The North Atlantic Treaty Organization, set up in 1949 by 11 Western countries to defend themselves against possible Communist attack.
neutral	A country that refuses, or is not allowed, to ally itself with any other country.
non-aligned	A country that refuses to align itself with either side in a dispute. From the 1950s onwards, Yugoslavia, Egypt, India and Indonesia led an international non-alignment movement that refused to take sides in the Cold War between East and West.
one-party state	A country in which only a single political party is allowed, which governs the country without any opposition.
Ostpolitik	The policy pursued by the West German Chancellor Willy Brandt to develop friendly relations with eastern Europe.
partisan	Member of an armed resistance group fighting inside a country against an invading or occupying army.
perestroika	The policy of "reconstruction" of the USSR pursued by Gorbachev.
Red Army	The Soviet army.
republic	A country, such as the USA or France, governed by an elected head of state called a President.
revolution	The overthrow of a government or a political system by the people, leading to a new system of government.
royalist	A person who believes in government by monarchy with a king or queen as head of state.
superpower	A country with vast military and economic power, such as the USA, the USSR and, in recent years, China.
treaty	A formal and binding agreement between two or more countries.
United Nations (UN)	World organization set up in 1945 to work for peace and co-operation in the world.
USSR	The Union of the Soviet Socialist Republics, or the Soviet Union, which existed from 1922–91; commonly known as Russia.
Warsaw Pact	Military alliance in eastern Europe, dominated by the USSR.

INDEX

A
Afghanistan 24, 25, 27
arms race 14
Austria 6, 8, 16, 28

B
Berlin 7, 11, 17, 28
 Airlift 11
 Wall 16-17, 28, 29
bombs, atomic 7, 13, 14
Brandt, Willy 23
Brezhnev, Leonid 22, 23, 26
Britain/British 6, 8, 11, 13, 14, 19, 22
Bulgaria 9, 28, 29

C
Castro, Fidel 18, 19
China 12, 13, 14, 16, 21, 22, 23
Churchill, Winston 7, 8, 9
Communism 6, 8, 9, 10, 11, 12, 16, 17,
 19, 20, 21, 23, 24, 25, 26, 27, 28, 29
Cuba 17, 18-19
Czechoslovakia 9, 16, 23, 28, 29

D
détente 22-23, 24, 25

E
Eastern Bloc *see* Europe, eastern
Europe 6, 7, 10, 11, 17, 23, 25, 27, 29
 eastern 6, 8, 9, 11, 13, 16, 17, 27,
 28, 29
 western 6, 11, 24

F
France 6, 7, 8, 11, 14, 20, 21, 22

G
Germany 6, 7, 8, 9, 11, 15
 East 16, 17, 23, 28, 29
 West 11, 23, 28, 29
glasnost 26-27
Gorbachev, Mikhail 26, 27, 28, 29
Greece 8, 10, 11

H
Ho Chi Minh 20, 21
Hungary 9, 16, 17, 28, 29

I
Iron Curtain 8, 9, 17, 28

J
Japan 6, 7, 12, 13, 20, 21

K
Kennedy, John 15, 17, 18, 19
Khrushchev, Nikita 16, 17
Korea 6, 12, 13
Korean War 12-13

M
MacArthur, General Douglas 13
Marshall Aid/Plan 9, 10, 11
missiles, nuclear 14, 15, 19, 24, 25, 27
Molotov, Vyacheslav 9
Moon, race to reach 15

N
NATO 9, 13, 24
Nixon, Richard 23, 24
nuclear test ban treaties 19, 22
nuclear weapons 14, 18, 19, 22, 25, 27

P
perestroika 26
Poland 9, 16, 23, 27, 28, 29

R
Reagan, Ronald 24, 25, 27
Romania 9, 16, 29
Roosevelt, Franklin 7, 13

S
satellites, artificial 14, 15
SALT Agreement 22, 25
South-East Asia 6, 19, 20, 21
Stalin, Josef 6, 7, 9, 14, 16, 17
START 25
"Star Wars" 25, 27

T
Thatcher, Margaret 26, 27
Truman, Harry 7, 8, 10, 13
Turkey 10, 19

U
UN 13, 17, 28
USA 6, 7, 8, 9, 10, 11, 12, 13, 14, 15, 17,
 18, 19, 21, 22, 23, 24, 25, 26, 27
USSR 6, 7, 8, 9, 11, 12, 13, 14, 15, 16,
 17, 18, 19, 21, 22, 23, 24, 25, 26,
 27, 29

V
Vietnam War 20-21, 23

W
Warsaw Pact 9, 17, 23
World War II 6-7, 8, 23

Y
Yeltsin, Boris 29
Yugoslavia 8, 16